Contents

An introduction to Hinduism 2

Divisions and denominations 4

ISKCON 6

Sacred writings 8

Shruti – the Vedas 10

Smriti 12

The Trimurti 1 14

The Trimurti 2 16

Deities 1 18

Deities 2 20

Teachers and leaders 22

What do Hindus believe? 24

Society 26

Symbols 1 28

Symbols 2 30

Worship 1 32

Worship 2 34

Festivals 1 36

Festivals 2 38

Festivals 3 40

Pilgrimage 42

Rites of passage 1 44

Rites of passage 2 46

Creation 1 48

Creation 2 50

Moral issues 1 52

Moral issues 2 54

Ultimate questions 1 56

Ultimate questions 2 58

Glossary 60

Index 62

An introduction to Hinduism

In this section you will:
- learn how Hinduism began and developed
- learn about Hindu populations around the world.

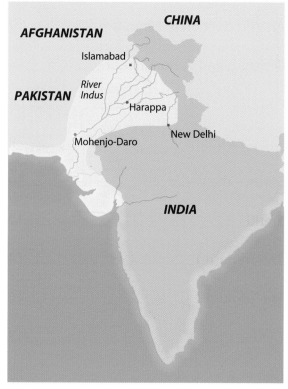

A map of India showing the area where Hinduism began and developed

What is Hinduism?

Hinduism is the oldest major world religion. It is the main religion of India but followers are found in many other countries. Altogether there are about 900 million Hindus. Many modern Hindus prefer to call their religion **Sanatan Dharma**, which means 'eternal or imperishable religion', because it is based on **divine** or God-given truths or laws, which have always existed. Hindus say their religion is also a way of life.

How did Hinduism begin and develop?

No one knows exactly when Hinduism began but most Hindus would agree it started in Northern India about 5000 years ago. It was not founded by one person or a group of people. It has developed over thousands of years starting with two ancient civilizations. These were the Dravidians who lived in the Indus Valley in Northern India and the Aryans who invaded India from the north. These people adopted many of each others' religious practices and beliefs, many of which are still seen in modern Hinduism.

Hindus have always been very tolerant of other religions. They believe and respect that there are many religions which lead to God. Hinduism is one way but followers of other religions may choose very different approaches and pathways to the same end.

Why is the religion called Hinduism?

There is more than one theory about where the words Hinduism and Hindu come from. Although the religion is many thousands of years old, many scholars think that the name Hinduism dates from

Religions Today

Hinduism

Pat Wootten

Heinemann
LIBRARY

www.heinemann.co.uk/library

Visit our website to find out more information about **Heinemann Library** books.

To order:
☎ Phone 44 (0) 1865 888066
🖨 Send a fax to 44 (0) 1865 314091
💻 Visit the Heinemann Bookshop at www.heinemann.co.uk/library to browse our catalogue and order online.

Heinemann Library
Halley Court, Jordan Hill, Oxford, OX2 8EJ
Part of Harcourt Limited

Heinemann is the registered trademark of
Harcourt Education Limited

Text © Pat Wootten, 2002

Original illustrations © Heinemann Educational
Publishers 2002

First published in 2002

ISBN 0 431 14975 5 (hardback)
06 05 04 03 02
10 9 8 7 6 5 4 3 2 1

ISBN 0 431 14982 8 (paperback)
07 06 05 04 03
10 9 8 7 6 5 4 3 2 1

British Library Cataloguing in Publication Data
A catalogue record for this book is available from the British Library

Picture research by Jennifer Johnson
Typeset by Artistix, Thame, Oxon
Illustrated by Andrew Skilleter
Printed and bound in Spain by Edelvives

Acknowledgements
The publishers would like to thank the following for permission to use photographs:

Andes Press Agency/Carlos Reyes-Manzo, p. 40 (left); The Art Archive/British Library, pp. 18 (left), 19; The Art Archive/Marco Polo Gallery Paris/Dagli Orti, p. 15; The Art Archive/Victoria and Albert Museum London, p. 16; Bhaktivedanta Manor, p. 53; Bruce Coleman Collection/Alain Compost, p. 29; Circa Photo Library, pp. 4, 5 (bottom), 6, 17, 40 (right); Circa Photo Library/William Holtby, pp. 23, 35; Circa Photo Library/Bipin J. Mistry, pp. 11, 25, 32; Circa Photo Library/John Smith, pp. 22, 38; Hulton Archive/Peter Ruhe, p. 55; Panos Pictures/James Bedding, p. 57; Science Photo Library/Francis Leroy, Biocosmos, p. 56; TRIP/Dinodia, p. 8; TRIP/F. Good, pp. 46, 47, 52; TRIP/R. Graham, p. 3; TRIP/S. Harris, p. 58; TRIP/H. Luther, pp. 39, 45; TRIP/H. Rogers, pp. 5 (top), 12, 14, 18 (right), 20 (both) 21 (bottom), 27, 28 (both), 29 (bottom), 30, 31, 34, 43.

The publishers have made every effort to contact copyright holders. However, if any material has been incorrectly acknowledged, the publishers would be pleased to correct this at the earliest opportunity.

Websites
Links to appropriate websites are given throughout the pack. Although these were up to date at the time of writing, it is essential for teachers to preview these sites before using them with pupils. This will ensure that the web address (URL) is still accurate and the content is suitable for your needs. We suggest that you bookmark useful sites and consider enabling pupils to access them through the school intranet. We are bringing this to your attention as we are aware of legitimate sites being appropriated illegally by people wanting to distribute unsuitable and offensive material. We strongly advise you to purchase suitable screening software so that pupils are protected from unsuitable sites and their material. If you do find that the links given no longer work, or the content is unsuitable, please let us know. Details of changes will be posted on our website.

Excavations showing the great bath at Moheryo-Dahb, an ancient settlement in the Indus Valley, northern India

about 1200 BCE when Persian invaders who were followers of Islam called the people who lived near the River Indus 'Sindhus'. Other scholars believe the word 'Hindu' comes from the name of the River Indus itself. Both of these theories refer to the area where the religion began and not to a founder or religious leader.

Hindus around the world

These are some of the largest Hindu populations in the world:

- India has 751 million Hindus.
- Nepal has more than seventeen million Hindus.
- Bangladesh has more than twelve million Hindus.
- Indonesia has four million Hindus.
- Sri Lanka has nearly three million Hindus.

Proportions of Hindus

The proportion of Hindus living in a country is different to the number of Hindus who live there. Countries which have only small populations may have a greater proportion of Hindus than countries which have large populations.

- 89 percent of people in Nepal are Hindu.
- Only 79 percent of Indians are Hindu.

Divisions and denominations

Who is a Hindu?

There are many different kinds of Hindus. They all share some common beliefs but there are also many different beliefs.

In 1995 the Indian Supreme court said a Hindu is someone who:

- accepts that the **Vedas** (**sacred** Hindu scriptures) contain the word of God

- recognizes that there are many different ways to know God

- realizes that there are a number of different **deities** (gods or goddesses) which can be worshipped.

What are the main divisions and denominations in Hinduism?

Hindus believe there is only one God, who they call **Brahman**. They believe that Brahman takes on many forms as gods or goddesses depending on what 'His' function is at the time. Most Hindus think one deity is more important than all the others and they choose to worship that deity more than the others. The group

they belong to depends upon which deity they have chosen to worship. Each group or **denomination** usually follows the teaching of a particular holy man who is called a **guru** or **swami**.

Hindus say it does not matter which deity, god or goddess you worship because you will reach Brahman the Supreme God through all of them.

Vaishnavism

About 80 per cent of Hindus choose to worship Vishnu in one of the forms he is believed to have appeared on earth. These forms are known as **avatars**. The most popular avatar is Krishna. Worshippers of Vishnu are called **Vaishnavas**.

Krishna, an avatar of Vishnu

Shiva, the deity of destruction and a reproductive power

Kali, a form of Shakti, the destructive and reproductive energy associated with Shiva

Shaivism

Hindus who choose to worship the deity Shiva are called **Shaivas**.

Shaktas

Hindus who choose to worship Shakta, the wife of Shiva, are called **Shaktas**. She has many different names and forms such as Devi, Mataji, Parvati, Durga, Kali and Amba. Shaktas may also worship other goddesses such as Lakshmi and Sarasvati.

In India most Hindus in cities or towns are either Vaishnavas, who worship Vishnu, or Shaivas, who worship Shiva. Hindus in the countryside tend to worship a goddess.

Facts about India

- India is the sixth largest country, and the largest democracy, in the world.
- More Hindus live in India than anywhere else in the world.
- India is one of the most ancient civilizations. European languages are based on the ancient Hindu language of Sanskrit.
- The world's first university was set up in Takshashila in about 700 BCE.
- The game of chess was invented in India.
- Our number system and the use of zero started in India.
- The art of navigation was developed in the River Sindhu about 6000 years ago.

ISKCON

In this section you will:

- learn about a Hindu centre in Britain, and the activities which take place there
- gain an understanding of why cows are sacred in Hinduism.

ISKCON

Many **Vaishnavas** belong to the International Society of **Krishna** Consciousness (**ISKCON**). The society was founded in New York in 1966 by A. C. Bhaktivedanta Swami Prabhupada to spread the message of **Hinduism** across the world. His teaching is based on two Hindu **sacred** writings, the **Bhagavad Gita** and the **Bhagavad Purana**.

In 1973, after studying with His Divine Grace, George Harrison, the ex-Beatle, became a Hindu and chose to become a

A. C. Bhaktivedanta Swami Prabhupada, the founder of ISKCON

follower of Krishna. He gave Bhaktivedanta Manor, near Watford in Hertfordshire, and the 28 hectares of land which surround it, to be the international centre for ISKCON.

Today Bhaktivedanta Manor is a holy place for Hindus dedicated to the teaching and spreading of Hinduism. On the estate there is a theological college where people can learn about Hinduism, a **mandir** where they can worship, a theatre where they can enjoy performances of many traditional art forms – such as dance – a working farm, which does not breed animals for food and gardens where they grow vegetables and plants. Some followers of Krishna live and work as part of the community but thousands more visit the manor regularly to study and worship. Hindu festivals are celebrated and some Hindus choose to hold important services such as weddings there. Visitors of all ages and beliefs are welcomed at the manor and many school children visit to learn about Hinduism. Making visitors feel welcome is an important part of being a Hindu.

The purpose of ISKCON is to spread the message of Hinduism (**Sanatan Dharma**) throughout the world. They have set up mandirs (temples) in most major cities as centres of worship and education and also as a retreat for those who want time away from their everyday lives to think and pray. The society is also known as the **Hare Krishna Movement**. This name comes from a **mantra**, which is a short religious saying or prayer that is chanted time and time again either as part of public worship or in private. Krishna is one of the **Sanskrit** names for God and means 'The All Attractive One'.

'Hare Krishna, Hare Krishna, Krishna, Krishna, Hare, Hare, Hare Rama, Hare Rama, Rama, Rama, Hare, Hare.'

Hindus believe that this chant contains God's holy names and by chanting them they will become pure and closer to God. This idea comes from the **Vedas**, which are sacred Hindu scriptures.

Sacred cows

Bhaktivedanta Manor runs a cow protection scheme. People can make donations to help to provide care for cows using animal-friendly methods, which have been used in India for thousands of years.

Hindus believe that cows are sacred creatures. They represent Mother Earth and, through their milk, symbolize all the wonderful gifts she gives to humans. Cows also symbolize the reverence that Hindus show for all living things, and feeding and caring for cows is seen as an act of worship. In India and other mainly Hindu countries, cows can be seen wandering the streets. No matter how much nuisance they create, they will never be harmed.

Sacred writings

In this section you will:
- learn about Hindu sacred writings and their sources
- read about the ancient language of Sanskrit.

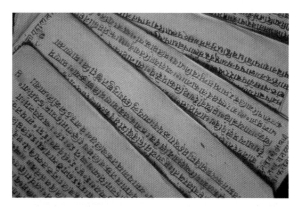

Hindu scriptures written in Sanskrit

In most other world faiths, such as Christianity and Judaism, scripture (sacred writings) has always played a very important part in teaching and learning about the faith.

In **Hinduism** scripture came into being thousands of years after the religion began and even then most of the scriptures were still passed on by word of mouth. Students listened to their teachers reciting the scriptures and copied not just what they said but also exactly how they said it, so that the words and the meaning stayed exactly the same. Hindus also believed that some scriptures were too holy to be written down and so for many centuries Hindus learnt about their faith only by listening to **gurus**, priests and sages (wise and holy men).

What are the Hindu sacred writings?

There are hundreds of sacred writings within Hinduism. Most were written originally in the ancient language of **Sanskrit**, which is no longer used in everyday life but is still used in religious practices. Most Hindus rely on their priests to translate the text for them, although many sacred texts have been translated into other languages such as Hindi, Gujurati and English. Each **denomination** in Hinduism has its own scriptures. Sacred texts written by followers of Shiva (**Shaivas**) were originally written in Tamil. The sacred writings are divided into two main categories: **shruti** and **smriti**.

Shruti

Shruti means 'that which is heard'. Hindus believe that these writings contain the words that God actually spoke to ancient sages and that they passed them on word for word. Hindus believe that God 'revealed' himself to humans through these words. The text has stayed the same for thousands of years because Hindus believe that God's words can never be changed.

Smriti

Smriti means 'that which has been remembered' and refers to texts that were written by ordinary people and tell of what they remember being told about God. Hindus have different opinions about

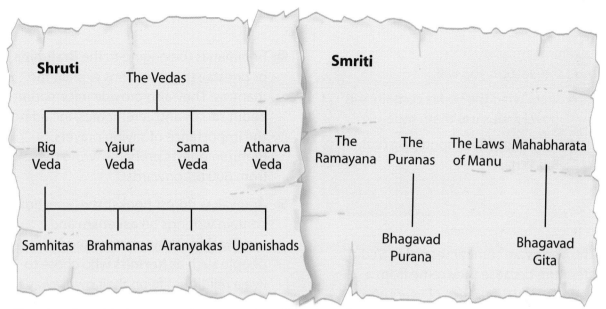

Shruti and smriti, the two main categories of Hindu scriptures

whether these texts are as important as shruti. The smriti text helps to explain the shruti and gives explanations and advice about how rituals are to be performed and includes the law and text on mythology and philosophy. Smriti texts have changed over time and are still being adapted to make them relevant to Hindus today.

In modern times, the Bhaktivedante Book Trust (BBT) which is part of ISCKON, has published some 500 million books and articles about Hinduism in 60 different languages. Many Hindus use smriti text to guide their everyday lives. The meaning of the text has stayed the same for thousands of years but modern interpretations help them to understand and experience God in today's world.

Sanskrit – the mother of languages

The ancient language of Sanskrit is the oldest known language still in use. Although today the language is read, written or recited mostly by scholars and religious leaders, it has been a living language for thousands of years. Sanskrit is the original language of many Hindu sacred writings, such as the **Vedas**, and is also used in religious ceremonies for prayers, **mantras** and hymns.

Sanskrit is a very rich language, and there are many different words meaning almost the same thing. For example, there are 70 root words for water. Prefixes can be added to these words to further explain the exact meaning, making 280 for water altogether! In modern times, computer programmers have been interested in using Sanskrit.

Shruti – the Vedas

In this section you will:

● learn what the Vedas contain and how Hindus use them today

● read and reflect upon part of the Rig Veda.

The **Vedas** are sometimes called Vedic literature because they came from a period many thousands of years ago called the Vedic period. The oldest part of the Vedas is the Rig Veda which contains 1028 hymns of praise. The earliest written version of the Rig Veda is thought to be dated as far back as the fifteenth century.

What are the Vedas?

The word Vedas comes from the **Sanskrit** word 'vid' meaning 'to know'. The Vedas is a collection of sacred writings, which Hindus believe are God's words as heard in the beginning by ancient wise and holy men.

What do the Vedas contain?

The Vedas is set out under four headings: the Rig Veda, Yajur Veda, Sama Veda and Atharva Veda. Each of the Vedas also has four parts. For centuries these sacred texts were learned by heart and passed on from generation to generation before they were written down.

1 Samhitas (**mantras**): these sections contain prayers and hymns, also called mantras. Some are more than 5000 years old.

2 Brahmanas (belonging to the **Brahmins**, or priests): these sections explain the mantras. They also provide information about rituals and ceremonies, including the importance of saying prayers. Brahmin priests probably wrote these from 600 BCE onwards.

3 Aranyakas (forest books): these sections contain writings on **ascetism** and **meditation**. They were written for people such as **hermits** who chose to live a religious life on their own, away from other people.

4 **Upanishads** (sitting down near): these sections contain discussions between holy men and their students about important Hindu beliefs, such as how the world began and the idea that God or **Brahman** is in everything as the **atman** or soul. Many Hindus find this section easier to understand than other parts of the Vedas. This is because other sections were only meant to be understood by the Brahmins. They are believed to have been written down between 600 and 200 BCE.

The Rig Veda mentions many different gods and goddesses, but one verse suggests that from the very beginning of **Hinduism** some followers believed that these **deities** were all forms of the one God, Brahman.

It is called Indra, Mitra, Varuna and Agni
And also Gautman the lovely-winged in heaven.
The real is one, though known by different names:
It is now called Agni, now Yama, now Matarishvan.

Rig Veda

*A Brahmin priest reading excerpts from the Vedas at Varanasi, a holy city on the banks of the **Ganga***

How do Hindus use the Vedas?

Hinduism is based on the teachings of the four Vedas, but many modern Hindus do not read them and the texts no longer play an important part in worship. The priest may sometimes read from a smaller book containing parts of the Vedas but usually, following the ancient tradition, he will chant or recite from memory. Verses from the Vedas are recited as mantras in important ceremonies such as the sacred thread ceremony and marriage. Listening to the priest recite sacred texts in Sanskrit is a very important part of worship for Hindus.

The Rig Veda

The Rig Veda is the oldest and most important section of the Vedas. It contains 1028 hymns of praise. The first hymn is in praise of Agni, the god of fire. Here are its opening lines:

'I extol Agni, the household priest, the divine minister of the sacrifice, the chief priest, the bestower of blessings.
May that Agni, who is to be extolled by ancient and modern seers, conduct the gods here.
Through Agni may one gain day by day wealth and welfare which is glorious and replete with heroic sons.'

From Rig Veda, I, 1

Smriti

In this section you will:
● learn about sacred writings called smriti and find out how they are used
● find out about the most popular sacred writings, and how they are used.

Smriti texts were written from about 500 BCE onwards. They include teaching and guidance on moral and religious issues and are believed to be the words of 'ordinary' people and not words directly spoken by God. Smriti means 'that which has been remembered'.

The Puranas

Purana means 'ancient', and the Puranas contain stories and legends from the very distant past. The Puranas focus on the main Hindu **deities** of Vishnu, Shiva and Brahma, but they also teach about morals and the right way to behave.

The oldest Purana was written in about 300 CE and the rest over the next 1000 years. This group of texts show how **Hinduism** has developed since the **Vedas** were written and much of modern Hinduism is based on what they say.

The Laws of Manu

The **Laws of Manu** is a collection of smriti law books that contain rules about how Hindus should live their lives. 'Manu' means

Krishna as a child, stealing milk from the butterchurn

'man' and according to Hindu mythology there were fourteen powerful 'Manus' who were our ancestors and ruled over the world for a period of time. The Laws of Manu were not written down until about 100 CE. Some of the laws regarding the treatment of women and some social groups have been questioned or criticized in modern times.

The Mahabharata and the Bhagavad Gita

The **Mahabharata** is also known as 'The Great Indian Epic'. It is the world's longest and perhaps greatest poem. It has three million words, 220,000 lines and 100,000 verses!

The main theme running through the epic is good versus evil and the story is told through two royal families who trick and fight against each other to gain control of the country. One of the main characters is **Krishna**. In one battle Krishna acts as a charioteer for Arjuna, one of the warring princes, and teaches the prince about war and life in general. This part of the Mahabharata is often printed in a separate book called the **Bhagavad Gita**, which is the most popular of all the Hindu sacred writings. 'Gita' means 'song' and 'Bhagavad' means 'adorable one', another name for God. This book is also known as 'The Song of God'.

The Mahabharata and Bhagavad Gita are important **sacred** texts. The stories explain how God wants people to live.

The Ramayana

The **Ramayana** is another epic poem, which tells the story of the adventures of Rama, who was the seventh **avatar** or incarnation of the god Vishnu. It explains the story of Rama and his wife Sita and emphasizes the value of courage and loyalty as well as keeping promises. This story shows a positive view of Hindu women and the sacrifices they make. The Ramayana helps Hindus to understand the teaching of the Vedas. It reminds them of

the right way to behave and that they have responsibilities towards other people. It gives them hope that good will always overcome evil. The Ramayana is retold or enacted every year at the festival of **Divali**.

Sacred texts

There are more than 400,000 Hindus in the UK. The most popular sacred writings for British Hindus are:

- the Mahabharata, the longest poem in the world, which contains the Bhagavad Gita

- the Bhagavad Gita, or 'The Song of the Lord', which was believed to have been spoken by Krishna

- the Bhagavad Purana (particularly the tenth chapter, which contains stories about Krishna)

- the Ramayana, a poem which tells the story of Rama and Sita.

Hindus treat their scripture with great respect. They always wash their hands before touching them and they are never placed on the floor. Prayers are sometimes said before reading them.

The Trimurti 1

In this section you will:

● learn what Hindus believe to be true about God

● find out how they represent God

● gain an understanding of Brahma, the creator god

● read about the importance of murtis, or images, in Hinduism, and the special way in which they are made.

How do Hindus understand God?

Hindus believe in One Supreme God who they call **Brahman**. They worship one God in many different forms, depending on the different functions they believe God performs. Hindus believe God is **omnipresent**, which means always present, everywhere and in all living things and can therefore be male or female. In **Hinduism**, therefore, God is worshipped in male and female forms as gods and goddesses. It teaches that men and women are 'different wings of the same bird'. Some Hindus believe that there are as many as 33 million different **deities**, all of which have a special function as part of Brahman.

The three main forms of God in Hinduism make up the **Trimurti**, 'three forms':

● Brahma, the creator

● Vishnu, the preserver

● Shiva, the destroyer.

The three gods of the Trimurti work together to keep the continuous cycle of life in the universe.

Some Hindus say that the three letters of GOD relate to these three main functions of Brahman:

G Generator, in the form of Brahma, the creator.

O Operator, in the form of Vishnu, who preserves and keeps things going.

D Destroyer, in the form of Shiva, who destroys in order for Brahma to re-create.

The Trimurti is sometimes depicted as a three-headed man. This symbolizes the Hindu belief that Brahma, Vishnu and Shiva are all aspects of One Supreme Being, Brahman

How do Hindus represent God?

The three-headed image of the Trimurti shows that Brahma, Vishnu and Shiva are all aspects of One Supreme Being – Brahman. Modern Hindus usually worship one individual aspect of Brahman.

Hindus represent God by visual images called **murtis** or by pictures. These images have symbolic superhuman features and carry objects, which show important Hindu beliefs and ideas about God.

Brahma, the creator of the universe

Brahma

Hinduism teaches that Brahma is the creator of the universe and all living things. Brahma is also believed to have created the sacred writings called the **Vedas**.

Brahma is shown with four heads, bearded faces and four arms. The heads allow him to see in all directions at once. This symbolizes that God is **omniscient**, or all-knowing. The four arms symbolize that God is **omnipotent**, or all-powerful. He usually carries some water, symbolizing his role as creator, and a spoon, which also acts as a sceptre to remind worshippers that he is divine and that they should make offerings when they worship. He also wears a string of beads, or **mala**, to remind them to pray, and a book to represent the Vedas.

Brahma is sometimes shown sitting on a **lotus flower**, which is a symbol of purity, with a white swan, which transports him.

Murtis

The Sanskrit word for image is murti. Murtis are the holiest objects in a **mandir** or Hindu home. Hindu scriptures contain texts, called Shilpashastras, which describe how a murti should be made. The Shilpashastras also contain rules about architecture and building cities. They are based on ancient artistic traditions.

The Hindu scriptures state: 'A murti when made in the correct proportions, its limbs and features neither too large or too small, may be called beautiful.' They also say that: '… the murti should not only be made as per the guidelines, but the sculptor should take care that the face conveys the beauty of the soul, pleasure, seriousness and strength.'

In this section you will:
● learn more about how Hindus represent God
● gain an understanding of the gods Vishnu and Shiva
● read about the Shiva linga.

Vishnu

Hindus believe that Vishnu is the preserver of the universe and protects the world from evil. He represents mercy and goodness and is always present everywhere and in everything. Hindus believe that when God chose to be seen he came to earth in

Vishnu, a member of the Trimurti, is believed to be responsible for preserving the universe

different forms. These are called incarnations or **avatars**. The most celebrated avatars are Rama and Krishna.

Vishnu is shown with a blue or dark blue skin colour to symbolize he is like the sky – everywhere and everlasting. Three vertical lines on his forehead symbolize that he is one of the **Trimurti**. He has four arms, which symbolize power. In one hand he holds a mace or club and in the other a discus, which represents the sun and is his magic weapon. In his other hands he holds a **lotus flower** as a sign of peace and a sacred white conch shell. In ancient times a conch shell was blown to start and end battles. Some Hindus believe the shell will keep away evil spirits and save human beings from disaster. Vishnu is sometimes shown seated on a huge serpent. Vishnu's vehicle is Garuda, the king of the birds, a half-man, half-eagle.

Shiva

Hinduism teaches that Shiva is the god of destruction but by destroying things he makes new life possible. His energy is called **Shakti** and this can destroy and recreate. Shakti takes on a female form as Shiva's consort or wife Parvati and as her avatars Durga and Kali.

Shiva is known by many other names and is shown in different ways. In one of the best-known forms he is shown as an ascetic – a holy man who chooses to live a very harsh life for religious reasons. He sits cross-legged on a tiger skin, deep in **meditation**. He wears a loincloth of antelope skin around his waist. The animal

'Shiva Nataraja', as 'Lord of the Dance'

standing on the dwarf of evil and ignorance. The flames symbolize Shakti or energy. They also remind Hindus of the fires of cremation following death.

skin symbolizes bravery and the fact that he can overcome his enemies. He has a crescent moon in his long matted hair and a topknot, out of which comes a symbol of the sacred River **Ganges**. Snakes are entwined in his hair and around his neck and arms. Three horizontal lines on his forehead show that he is part of the Trimurti.

Shiva has a blue throat because, legend says, he drank poison from the ocean to save the world from destruction. His three eyes enable him to see past, present and future. The third eye in the middle of his forehead is closed unless it is used to destroy evil. He holds a three-pronged spear, which represents the Trimurti. His vehicle is Nandi, the white bull.

Another popular image of Shiva is as Nataraja or 'Lord of the Dance'. Here he is shown dancing in a circle of flames and

The Shiva linga

Shiva is also represented by the linga, which is a column of stone or metal. In some Hindu temples, the Shiva linga is the main deity. During worship, followers of Shiva pour liquids, such as water, milk or honey, over the Shiva linga, whilst prayers are said.

One example of a Shiva linga

Deities 1

In this section you will:

- learn about some deities, or gods and goddesses
- read about the story of the birth of Krishna.

Gods and goddesses

Images of Hindu **deities**, or gods and goddesses, show that these are far more than human. They do not show what they actually look like but symbolize their power or wisdom. For example, they can be shown with many arms or a third eye

*Rama, his wife Sita and companions. The story of the Ramayana is remembered during the festivals of **Divali** and Dassehra*

like Shiva. Each god has a wife or a consort. This shows that the Supreme Being, **Brahman**, is male and female.

Hindus believe that the god Vishnu has been to earth nine times in different forms. Hindus call these 'visits' **avatars**.

Rama

Rama is the seventh avatar of Vishnu. Hindus believe that Rama came to earth in order to defeat a wicked demon and show humans how to live. The story is told in the **Ramayana**, one of the **sacred** Hindu texts. Rama is shown as a human being with blue skin and marks on his forehead like Vishnu. He carries a bow and has a quiver full of arrows on his back.

Lakshmi is worshipped during the festival of Divali

Krishna

Krishna is the eighth avatar of Vishnu. He is shown in human form with blue skin. Krishna carries a flute, wears a peacock feather in his hair and is often shown with a white cow. He is known for beauty, mischief and fun, as well as great wisdom.

Lakshmi

Lakshmi is the wife or consort of Vishnu. She is the goddess of happiness, wealth and good fortune and is usually shown on a **lotus flower** with elephants on either side of her.

Parvati

Parvati is Shiva's wife or consort. She is gentle and peace-loving and concerned with family in the form of **Shakti** or Devi, but she also has a more fearsome side. Parvati is worshipped by Hindu women in the hope of a happy married life. Shiva and Parvati are also the parents of Ganesha, the elephant-headed God.

The birth of Krishna

The demon King Kamsa believed that his sister, Devaki, would have a child who would kill him. So he threw her and her husband, Vasudeva, in prison, and killed all their children. However, when Krishna was born, he told his father to exchange him for the child of a cowherd called Nanda, who lived across the River Yamuna. Then his father's chains fell off, the prison doors opened and the guards fell asleep. Vasudeva exchanged Krishna for the cowherd's daughter, and took her back to prison. His chains fastened together once more, the prison doors locked and the guards woke up. They told Kamsa that another child had been born but, when he came to kill it, the child stood up and said she was the goddess Yogamaya, and that Devaki's baby, Krishna, was alive and would one day return to kill him.

Parvati holding Ganesha

Deities 2

In this section you will:

- learn more about Hindu deities, or gods and goddesses
- read and reflect upon some prayers to Ganesha.

Durga

Durga is a fierce and powerful form of **Shakti** or Devi. She rides on a lion and carries many objects, including weapons, in her hands. Legend says that her strength and weapons were given to her by the gods who needed her help to defeat a cunning buffalo demon.

*Saraswati is usually worshipped during the festival of Vasanta Panchami, also known as Saraswati **Puja**. The festival marks the beginning of spring*

Saraswati

Saraswati is the wife or consort of Brahma. She is the goddess of learning and the arts. This beautiful pale-skinned goddess is dressed in fine clothes. Her four arms represent four aspects of the human personality: intelligence, understanding, self-esteem and sense of right and wrong. She usually carries a stringed musical instrument, a copy of the **Vedas** and a **mala**. The white swan of Brahma or a peacock is her vehicle.

Durga is worshipped during the festival of Navaratri

Ganesha

Ganesha has an elephant head. He is the god of wisdom and good fortune and known as 'the remover of obstacles'. Hindus pray to Ganesha for good luck before they pray to other gods and goddesses. He is shown on greetings cards for celebrations such as births and weddings. Ganesha has a round stomach and holds a dish of sweets symbolizing prosperity. One of his other hands gives a blessing to his followers, and another holds a **lotus flower**. He carries an axe to remove obstacles. His companion is a black rat, which symbolizes that all creatures are valued and have a purpose.

The Hindu festival of Ganesh-Chaturthi celebrates Ganesha's birthday

Kali

Shiva's Shakti energy is seen in Kali, another form of Parvati. As Kali she is a fierce and powerful form of mother nature and a reminder that power should be admired, respected and feared. Kali wears a necklace of skulls and severed arms hang from her waist. Her tongue is often shown hanging out with the blood of her victims dripping from it. She might hold a severed head in one hand and a sickle (a deadly weapon) in another. Kali looks fearsome, but she gives peace by helping her followers to fight their demons.

Prayers to Ganesha

Hindus pray to Ganesha regularly at home and in the mandir. They will often pray to Ganesha before they pray to their own chosen deity, and prayers to the elephant-headed god are included in many religious ceremonies. Here is an example of a prayer to Ganesha.

'Maker of happiness, remover of miseries, whose grace extends love to us and does not leave a trace of any obstacle remaining, you have a layer of red lead around your whole body and a necklace of pearls shines brightly around your neck. Victory to you, victory to you, O god of auspicious form. At your sight, all desires of the mind are fulfilled.'

Teachers and leaders

In this section you will:

● learn about some of the teachers and leaders in Hinduism, and what they do

● gain an understanding of how Hindus learn through storytelling.

Hindus listening to a story from scripture. The storyteller often knows large portions of the scripture by heart, and will adapt stories to suit their audience

The mandir priests

Every **mandir** or temple has its own priest or staff of priests. It takes a long time to become a priest. They must have detailed knowledge of the **sacred** writings, teachings and practices of **Hinduism** and be able to show that they are in control of their body and their mind. Some priests are also trained astrologers.

Two of the most important roles of a priest are to conduct religious ceremonies and care for the **shrines** in the mandir. The priest must wash and dress the images of the gods and goddesses, the **murtis**, every morning. This shows respect for **Brahman** and purifies the shrine. The priest must also purify himself on the inside and on the outside before worship can take place. He does this by washing or bathing, ideally in a sacred pool or river, and by studying sacred writings, meditating or doing yoga.

The guru

A **guru** is a special kind of spiritual teacher who helps people to learn more about themselves and develop their relationship with God. A guru helps people to understand and carry out their religious duties. Hindus believe that gurus have the power to help them reach **moksha**, which frees them from the cycle of life and death. Some followers or disciples spend years studying with their guru, others may never see or meet him but will have a picture of their chosen Guru and study his writings. Many Hindu shrines have pictures of gurus and they are shown great respect.

Sathya Sai Baba

Sathya Sai Baba is a very popular modern Indian guru. Millions of Hindus believe he is an **avatar** of God. Every day thousands of his followers wait at his **ashram**, a place set up for spiritual development, hoping to see or hear him. Sai Baba is committed to respect for all religions and religious unity for world peace. This is shown in the universal symbol he has produced, which combines all the symbols of the major world religions.

Sathya Sai Baba announced his mission in 1940. Every day, for more than 50 years, he has walked among and talked to pilgrims who come to see him

The storytellers

Storytelling is an important way in which Hindus learn about their faith and what is expected of them. Many storytellers can recite large portions of scripture from memory but adapt the stories to suit their audience. Hindus enjoy hearing the same stories repeated over and over again. They never get bored because the stories have many different levels of meaning, which help them to make sense of their own lives.

Sai Baba's universal symbol

Hindu teachers and leaders

In the past 100 years, there have been many great teachers and leaders.

● Shri Aurobindo developed yoga, which helped people to clear their minds to think about God.

● Mahatma Gandhi is famous for his passive resistance to British rule in India, and his stand against the caste system.

● Sathya Sai Baba is a famous modern guru, based in India.

● A. C. Bhaktivedante Swami Prabhupada founded ISKCON.

● Pramukh Swami is the leader of the Swaminarayans in Neasden, London.

What do Hindus believe?

In this section you will:

- learn about some important Hindu beliefs and how Hindus develop their spiritual lives
- read about the vows that some followers of Krishna take.

There are a wide range of different beliefs and practices within **Hinduism**. However, there is a set of basic beliefs which most Hindus share.

Hindus believe in One Supreme God, whom they call **Brahman**, but they worship Brahman in many different forms because of the many functions He performs. Brahman is all-seeing, all-knowing and ever-present. Hindus say God has always existed and always will exist. Part of Brahman, called the **atman** or soul, is in all living things.

Hindus believe that we should not bother about material things, such as what we own or wear, because none of these last for ever.

They are **finite** and what is important to us today may not be tomorrow. Hindus say the only thing which is permanent is the atman or soul, which does last forever.

Samsara

Hindus believe in **transmigration**. This means that when a person dies, the atman or soul enters a new body and takes on a different form to continue the cycle of birth, death and rebirth, which they call **samsara** or **reincarnation**. This may mean that the atman lives on through many lives and in the form of a variety of species. The aim of every Hindu is to achieve **moksha**. This is when the atman no longer needs to be reborn but is pure and free to return to Brahman.

Karma

Hindus believe in **karma**, which is also known as 'the law of cause and effect'. This means that if they live a good life and carry out their religious duties, their next

Agami karma: all the echoes performed in this life will affect the future. Good actions can help reduce suffering. Bad actions can increase suffering

*A **Brahmin** practising yoga*

The greatest dharma, or religious duty, for a Hindu is to practise **ahimsa**, which means 'non-killing' or 'non-violence'. This means that Hindus must respect all life. Most Hindus are vegetarians because of following ahimsa. They believe all living things should be allowed to live out their natural life span and not be killed for food.

Religious commitment

Some followers of Krishna, called devotees, make lifelong vows. They promise that they will:

● not eat fish, meat or eggs

● not take any artificial stimulants (including tea, coffee and tobacco)

● not take part in gambling

● only have sexual intercourse when they are married and want children.

They promise to meditate every day by chanting the Hare Krishna mantra and counting on a **mala**, a necklace of 108 wooden beads which form a circle.

Devotees in a religious community such as ISKCON start the day with worship at 4.30 a.m. Many of the men shave their heads. They wear orange or white traditional robes, called dhotis. The colour depends on whether they are monks, or single or married men. The women wear saris. Devotees usually wear a marking on their forehead, called a tilak. The community meets again for worship at 7.00 p.m.

life will be better than the one they have now. But if they live a selfish, wicked life, the consequences are that they will be reborn into a life which will not be as good as the one they have now.

Spiritual development

Hindus believe they must perform **dharma**, that is, fulfil their religious duties by worshipping at home as well as in the **mandir** and by taking part in religious rituals throughout their lives. They believe they must work towards being pure in body and in mind. Purifying the body is done by ritual bathing in **sacred** water such as a river. Purifying the mind is done through **meditation** and yoga or through following the spiritual advice and teachings of a **guru**.

Society

In this section you will:

- learn about how Hindu Indian society has been organized
- find out about the groups called jatis, or castes
- read about the 'untouchables'.

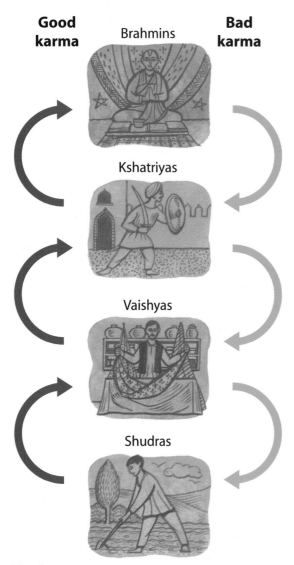

Good karma

Bad karma

Brahmins

Kshatriyas

Vaishyas

Shudras

The four varnas

How is Hindu society organized?

Traditionally, Indian society has been divided into four main classes, called **varnas**. Each varna is linked to particular jobs or occupations and has a status that goes with it. The higher the varna, the closer to God people were thought to be.

Brahmins, who were the priests and advisers, were the first and most important varna. Then came the **Kshatriyas**, who were soldiers and rulers. Next came the **Vaishyas**, who were shopkeepers, traders, farmers and skilled workers. Lastly came the **Shudras**, who were unskilled workers and worked for the other three varnas. Over time, these four varnas divided up into thousands of sub-groups called **jatis** or **castes**. A jati or caste was made up of families who all followed the same occupation. This became called the **caste system**.

There were people who did not belong to any of the four main varnas. These people did the dirtiest and most unpleasant jobs and were not allowed to worship or mix with people from the three highest varnas. They were called the **untouchables**. In modern times the rigid caste system is more flexible and in 1950 temples became open to all Hindus.

Many Hindus believe that the jati or caste you are born into depends on how you lived a previous life. The idea that the consequences of your thoughts and actions are carried forward from one life to the next is called **samchita karma**.

According to one Hindu creation story, the varnas came into being from the first man, who was called **Purusha**. The Brahmins

Members of an unskilled jati decorating pots in India

(priests) came from his mouth, the Kshatriyas (soldiers or rulers) from his arms, the Vaishyas (shopkeepers, traders and farmers) from his thighs and the Shudras (unskilled workers) from his feet.

In the past, Hindus could only mix with people in the same jati or caste and had to do the jobs their families had always done. People from different castes could not marry each other. Things are more flexible now, but the caste system still exists.

The 'untouchables'

The 'untouchables', now called Dalits, are Hindus who do not belong to the four main castes. Traditionally, they have done all the most unpleasant jobs, such as:

● dealing with dead animals, including tanning leather

● cleaning up human sewage and animal manure.

Characteristics of different varnas

The **Bhagavad Gita** describes some of the qualities of different varnas, such as:

'Peacefulness, self-control, austerity, purity, tolerance, honesty, knowledge, wisdom and religiousness – these are the natural qualities by which the Brahmanas work.'

Bhagavad Gita, 18, 43

Symbols 1

In this section you will:
● learn about some Hindu symbols and their use in religious life
● read about the sacredness of the colour saffron in Hinduism.

Symbolism is very important in **Hinduism**. It affects the way Hindus worship, the objects they use, what they do and the words they use to describe God. All of the gods and goddesses are symbols of a different aspect of the One Supreme God, **Brahman**. Many have supernatural features, such as several pairs of arms, and carry symbolic objects to show their particular qualities and the aspect of Brahman they represent. Hindu sacred writings and stories are full of symbolism.

Aum

Aum, sometimes spelt **Om**, is the main symbol of Hinduism. Aum is a **sacred** sound for Hindus. They believe it is the first sound that God made and that all other sounds including speech came from it. It is the sound of creation. Aum is said in chants and **meditations** and Hindus say repeating it helps them to relax and feel comfort, blessings and peace.

Aum: the imperishable syllable

The swastika

The word **swastika** comes from the **Sanskrit** word for 'well-being'. Hindus believe the swastika represents good luck. They sometimes draw it on the front page of account books or on the floor of their house during festivals and use it in other important ceremonies, such as weddings.

*A rangoli pattern using the swastika, made for the festival of **Divali***

The four arms of the swastika are thought to represent:

- space – the four points of the compass, north, south, east and west.
- time – the four ashramas (stages of life).
- knowledge – the four vedas.

The coconut

The coconut has more than one symbolic meaning. The three dots around the base can represent the **Trimurti**, the three main forms of Brahman. They can also symbolize the belief that humans have three eyes, two which they see with and a third 'inner eye' which is their conscience.

Because the fruit inside the coconut is white and untouched by human hands Hindus believe it is the purest form of offering they can give to God and they often use it in ceremonies to signify purity, fertility and blessing. Hindu wedding invitations are often decorated with important symbols such as the swastika and coconut.

The coconut is used frequently during religious ceremonies

The lotus flower

The lotus: a symbol of good overcoming evil

The lotus symbolizes purity and goodness because, although it grows in muddy water, the flowers are clean and pure. Some of the gods and goddesses are shown sitting or standing on a **lotus flower** symbolizing that the evil in the world has no power over them.

Colour as a symbol

The colour saffron is made from a plant called Autumn Crocus, which grew in the Himalayan mountains. The orange/gold dye was expensive to produce and was considered very valuable.

Saffron is a sacred colour for Hindus. It is the colour of fire, which is used in worship to symbolize God. Hindu monks wear saffron robes to symbolize that they have given up all worldly possessions, and have dedicated their lives to learning about and serving God. Many Hindu temples fly triangular saffron flags to symbolize the fire, which holy men used to carry from place to place.

Symbols 2

In this section you will:
- learn about more Hindu symbols and their meanings and use
- read about the use of tilaka, or body markings, by different Hindu groups.

Ash

Some Hindus use ash to put marks on their foreheads. This symbolizes that only the **atman** or soul will last forever and that everything else is short-lived. The ash also reminds Hindus that life is short and that they must live their lives to show respect for all living things and that cremation follows death.

Sindoora

Hindu married women sometimes put a red mark in the parting of their hair. This symbolizes the power of the Mother Goddess, the female part of **Brahman**. They hope the Mother Goddess will protect their husbands and grant them a long life.

Bindi

The bindi is a red dot, put on the forehead during worship and worn as protection and blessing for married women and their husbands. The bindi represents the power of the Mother Goddess and the third eye of Shiva.

*Shaktas, **devotees** of the Mother Goddess, apply a round or slightly elongated red mark to their foreheads*

Hindus bathing in the River Ganges at Varanasi, India

Water

In **Hinduism**, water is an important symbol as a source of life. Newborn babies are washed at birth and the sacred symbol of **Aum** is traced on their lips. Hindus wash or bathe before worship as a symbol of purification. A jar of water is sometimes placed on a pile of corn outside the house of newlyweds in the hope they will be blessed with children. Sometimes holy water is sprinkled on the ground to remove evil.

There are seven **sacred** rivers. The most important of these is the River **Ganges**. Many legends are told about the River Ganges and Hindus believe it has amazing properties. One of these is that the water does not go stale even when it has been bottled for some time. Hindu scripture says that anywhere the River Ganges flows is sacred or holy and millions of people bathe in it as often as they can and take water home in jars to place in their household shrines.

Tilaka

Tilaka is the name given by Hindus to body markings which show which **denomination** they belong to.

Followers of Vishnu draw three vertical lines on their foreheads. This symbolizes Vishnu as part of the **Trimurti**, as well as their belief in Vishnu's power to protect and preserve things.

Worshippers of Shiva use ash to draw three horizontal lines on their foreheads. This symbolizes Shiva's role in the Trimurti, and the belief his followers have in his power to destroy and recreate things.

The followers of Shakti draw a round or slightly oval red mark on their foreheads. This symbolizes their belief in the power of the Mother Goddess.

In this section you will:
- learn how and why Hindus worship at home
- gain an understanding of Kathakali, a form of dance drama.

How do Hindus worship?

Hindus worship to show that **Brahman**, God, is important to them. It is part of their **dharma** or religious duty. Hindus believe that God is present in everything, this means that their everyday lives can be an act of worship. Taking part in worship in the home is part of their daily routine. All forms of worship are called **puja** by Hindus and the rituals which must be followed are written down in the **Vedas**.

Worship in the home

Hindu homes usually have a small shrine, which is used for family puja or worship. The shrine is beautifully decorated with flowers, jewellery, coins, tinsel and sometimes small coloured lights. In place of honour stands the **murti**, which is the family's chosen god or goddess. The murti is a representation of Brahman and is treated with great care and respect. This means that the murti is washed and 'dressed' everyday. Sometimes there are other murtis or pictures of **gurus** or important leaders in the shrine. One of these is Ganesha, the remover of obstacles, who is worshipped before all the other gods and goddesses. Other

items in the shrine show that puja involves the five senses and are symbols of the five elements of the universe: earth, air, fire, water and ether.

Many Hindus will take part in puja at least once a day. They may get up early and shower or bathe and spend some time in prayer, **meditation**, chanting or studying **sacred** writings before taking part in formal worship or puja. The mother or wife of the family usually performs the puja. The family members will not wear shoes as a sign of respect and will stand or sit in front of the shrine.

The puja may involve saying prayers, repeating **mantras**, and making offerings such as flowers. It may end with a special

A Hindu family shrine in the UK

- A bell is rung to let the deity know that worship is about to start. Hindus believe that Brahman cannot be expected to be just waiting around for us all the time.

- Ash, sandalwood paste or red dye is used to mark worshippers' foreheads as a symbol of their worship and the blessings and protection of Brahman.

- Food such as rice, nuts, sweets and fruit are offered to show how grateful they are for the love that God shows them.

- Water is sprinkled from a special spoon to symbolize the removal of evil. Sometimes this is holy water from a sacred river such as the **Ganges**.

- Incense is lit to purify and 'make holy' the air where prayers are being said.

- An arti lamp, which has five wicks symbolizing the five elements of the universe, is lit and moved in circles near the worshippers. Hindus believe that sacred fire can bring blessings from God.

A puja tray

ritual called **arti**, which means that the worshippers receive a blessing from the flames of the arti lamp as it is moved in a circle near them.

Kathakali lessons

Kathakali plays are designed to teach the audience important moral and religious lessons. The plays focus on personal and social issues, such as:

- Devotion
- Failure
- Forgiveness
- Love
- Society
- War

Kathakali

Kathakali is a form of classical dance drama performed by men. It started more than 400 years ago in Kerala in southern India. The performers 'tell' sacred stories through music and movement. In Kerala today, when the plays are performed, it is a time for great celebration. Everyone dresses in their best clothes, including the elephants, which are decorated with gold ornaments. They all take part in a procession to the temple. Today, you may be lucky enough to see a Kathakali performance by a troupe who travel the world to show their art.

In this section you will:
- learn how Hindus worship in the mandir
- think about the symbolism of offerings in worship
- read about Hindu temples in Britain.

Worship in the mandir

Although almost every Hindu home contains a simple shrine for family worship, the **mandir** is especially important because it is believed to be 'the home of God'. When Hindus worship in the mandir they believe they can make direct contact with God.

In India, there are thousands of purpose-built mandirs. Some are very big and include several buildings; others may be just a roadside shrine. In countries such as Britain mandirs are usually buildings that were once used for other things, although some Hindu communities have built their own. In a large mandir there may be several shrines, with the most popular **deity** having the central position. There are set times for services and some Hindus may go to the mandir every day whereas others may go only when there is a festival. Worshippers bring offerings such as flowers, milk, food, honey or money, and take off their shoes before they go into the central hall where worship takes place. Mandirs are also important meeting places for Hindus. They can go there to learn about their faith and also to enjoy social gatherings.

When Hindus take part in worship at the mandir there are three main aspects of the service. These are **havan**, **arti** and **bhajans**.

Havan

Havan is when the priest makes a small **sacred** fire from ghee (purified butter), **camphor**, wood, grains and seeds and offers it to the deities. He then takes some holy water in his left hand, dips a finger from his right hand into it and touches his ears, nose, mouth, arms, body and legs as a symbol of purification. Other worshippers do the same while the priest says prayers asking for power to be given to the five senses and to the limbs. Other prayers are

The Dakshineshwar Kali Temple in Calcutta, India

Hindus in India taking a blessing from the sacred flame during arti

said for the well-being of worshippers and prayers are offered to the main deities.

Arti

Arti is a ceremony in which love and devotion is offered to the deity and worshippers receive blessings in return. Symbols used during arti represent the five elements of the universe. A conch shell filled with water is blown at the start of the ceremony to symbolize water and ether. Offerings of flowers and incense represent the earth and a fan is waved to symbolize air. The five lights of the arti lamp represent fire. The arti lamp takes on power and blessings when it is moved in front of the deities and this is then transferred to the worshippers. They cup their hands over the flame and then pass their hands over their eyes, forehead and

hair. They usually make an offering of money in return for the blessing.

Bhajans

Bhajans are hymns or songs used in worship. Musical instruments are played to accompany the voices and worshippers clap their hands in time to the music. Dance is another important form of worship and many young Hindus take dance lessons. Professional dance troupes perform dramatizations of stories from **sacred** writings.

Hindu temples in Britain

Hindus live all over Britain, and some will travel long distances to their nearest temple. The temple is not just a place of worship, but is also a social meeting place. Families and friends arrange to meet there, and share news of other friends and relatives.

Many temples conduct language classes where young people who speak English as a first language can learn to speak, read and write Hindi, Gujurati or Bengali, which may be their parents' or grandparents' first language. Some temples provide opportunities for children to learn to play classical Indian instruments, such as the sitar, or hold classes in classical Indian dance. Family ceremonies and celebrations, such as weddings and sacred thread ceremonies, also take place in the temple.

Festivals 1

In this section you will:
- learn about the Hindu calendar
- find out about astrology and Hinduism
- read about seasons in India.

How is the Hindu calendar organized?

Hinduism has its own calendar. It is used to find out the dates of festivals and the best times to perform certain ceremonies. In 1957 the Indian Government set up a national calendar. Before this date Hindus used several different calendars depending on where in India they lived. The calendar is based on the movements of the sun and moon and is made of three parts, which overlap and connect together.

The solar year

The solar year lasts for 365 days and has twelve months. A leap year has 366 days. One solar month is the time it takes for the sun to move from one sign of the zodiac, or **rashi**, to another.

The lunar year

The lunar year is made up of twelve months but is eleven days shorter than a solar year. This is because it only takes the moon about 29 days to travel around the earth. For Hindus this means that every three years there is an extra month.

A lunar month is divided into two. It starts with a new moon. As it waxes and becomes more visible, Hindus call this time 'bright fortnight' and they believe it is a good time to get things done. The second half of the month, as the moon wanes and becomes less visible, is called 'dark fortnight' and is not such a good time to do things. The dates for most Hindu festivals are decided according to the phases of the moon.

March/April	Chaitra
April/May	Vaisakha
May/June	Jyeshtha
June/July	Ashada
July/August	Shravan
August/September	Bhadrapad
September/October	Ashvin
October/November	Kartik
November/December	Margashirsha
December/January	Pausha
January/February	Magha
February/March	Phalguna

Rashis: the signs of the zodiac

What role does astrology play in a Hindu's life?

Many Hindus believe that their lives are affected by the position of the stars and planets at the time they were born.

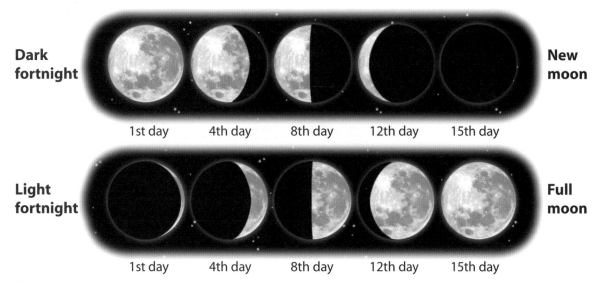

Dark fortnight — 1st day, 4th day, 8th day, 12th day, 15th day — New moon

Light fortnight — 1st day, 4th day, 8th day, 12th day, 15th day — Full moon

The phases of the moon

When a baby is born an astrologer draws up a horoscope or **Janmapatri**. Hindus believe that the horoscope will show when good things will happen and when life may get tough. It provides information about their character, what job they will do and how many children they will have. It is also used to find the right name for a child and checked to see whether a bride and groom will get on together.

When marriage is being considered, traditional Hindu parents may ask the astrologer to study the horoscopes of the bride and groom to see whether they are compatible. They may also ask the astrologer for advice about when would be an auspicious time for the wedding to take place, which means when would the marriage be most likely to be blessed. In India most Hindu weddings take place between December and July before the heavy monsoon rains begin and away from the major festivals such as **Divali**.

Seasons and festivals in India

In India, a solar year is divided into six seasons, each lasting two months and based on the weather.

- Vasanta (March/April) is spring. The festival of Holi marks the start of Vasanta.

- Grishma (May/June) is summer, and time for the festival of Akshaya Tritiya.

- Varsha (July/August) is the rainy season, when the festival of Raksha Bandhan takes place.

- Sharad (September/October) is autumn, when the festival of Dassehra takes place.

- Hemanta (November/December) is winter, when Divali takes place.

- Shishira (January/February) is the cool season, and time for the festival of Makara Sankrati.

Festivals 2

In this section you will:

● learn about some important Hindu festivals

● think about the importance and value of festivals.

Which festivals do Hindus celebrate?

There are many festivals in **Hinduism**. Some are more important than others depending on where you live or which **deity** you choose to worship. Festivals are based on stories in Hindu **sacred** writings and are very joyful occasions. There is also a serious side because the stories have important religious and moral meanings. Most festivals take place once a year and involve worship (**puja**).

Divali

Divali, the festival of lights, is one of the most important festivals. It takes place in the lunar month of Kartik (October–November) and is the start of the Hindu New Year, which is also their financial year. Many Hindus see Divali as a time to start again. They try to make up any quarrels or arguments they have had and to pay all their bills so they do not start the New Year in debt. Some Hindus may consult astrologers to find out what the year ahead has in store for them.

Divali celebrates that good will always overcome evil. The **Ramayana**, which tells the story of Prince Rama (an **avatar** of Vishnu) overcoming the demon Ravana to rescue his wife Sita, is a much-loved story told at Divali.

At Divali Hindus give their houses a special clean and decorate them with coloured

A Hindu shrine lit up for Divali

During Navaratri, worshippers perform a variety of dances, some using sticks

electric lights or **diva** lamps, which are small clay lamps filled with oil and a floating cottonwool wick. They make special sweet things to eat and create **rangoli** patterns on the doorstep or floor of the house. This is believed to encourage Lakshmi, the goddess of good fortune, to visit and bring good luck for the coming year.

Navaratri

Navaratri takes place in the month of Ashvin (September–October) and lasts for nine nights. This festival is dedicated to the Mother Goddess in the form of Durga. Every night during the festival worshippers go to the **mandir** and dance around a **shrine** dedicated to the goddess. The evening ends with an **arti** ceremony and sharing **prashad**, which is a mixture of foods that have been blessed. Some Hindus **fast** during the festival and eat only fruit or foods made with milk.

Dassehra

The festival of Dassehra follows straight after Navarati and means 'tenth day'. The **murti** of Durga is taken to a nearby river and symbolically washed. Hindus believe this washes away all their unhappiness and bad luck. They believe that Durga can overcome evil and help them to live happier lives. Large images of the demon Ravana from the story of Rama and Sita are sometimes burned at this time. This shows Rama's victory over the demon king and symbolizes good overcoming evil.

Holi

This joyful festival welcomes spring, and takes place on the full moon in the month of Phalguna (February/March). Bonfires are lit, and parents carry small children and babies around the fire to receive a blessing from the god of fire, Agni. Everyone has fun and, sometimes, children throw coloured powder at each other and unsuspecting adults.

Chaturthi

This festival celebrates the birth of Ganesha, the elephant-headed god of wisdom and good fortune, who is also known as the remover of obstacles. Clay images, or **murtis**, of Ganesha are specially made, and are worshipped during the festival, which lasts seven to ten days. On the last day, there is a joyful procession, and worshippers sing **bhajans** and dance as they take the murtis to a river or water source to be immersed.

Festivals 3

In this section you will:
- learn more about important Hindu festivals
- read and reflect upon a story about the festival of Kumbh Mela.

Janmashtami

The festival of Janmashtami takes place on the eighth day of Sravana (July–August) and celebrates the birthday of Krishna, the eighth **avatar** of Vishnu.

Images of the baby Krishna are placed in cradles and swings in the **mandir** and in Hindu homes. Hindus **fast** and stay up until midnight because they believe that is when Krishna was born. At midnight they gather around the cradle or swing, sing **bhajans**, dance and offer the 'baby' gifts of food and sweets. This is followed by an **arti** ceremony and then everyone shares **prashad**, the mixture of sweet foods that has been blessed. Some mandirs organize non-stop readings of the **Bhagavad Gita** for eight days before the festival. The readings are timed to finish at exactly midnight.

Raksha Bandhan

The festival of Raksha Bandhan also takes place during the month of Sravana. This is

A cradle containing a murti of the infant Krishna

A young Hindu girl ties a rakhi on her brother's wrist during Raksha Bandhan

when sisters tie a coloured silk or cotton bracelet called a **rakhi** around the wrist of their brothers, or male cousins if they do not have a brother, to say thank you for all the love and protection they have been given. They are usually given a present in return. In some Hindu communities a girl can tie a rakhi on any man's wrist and ask them to protect them. Rakhis are often sent to male relatives who live in other countries as a token of affection.

Makara Sankranti

'Makara' means 'Capricorn' and 'Sankranti' refers to when the sun passes from one zodiac sign to the next. This festival takes place around 14 January. The exact date depends on when the sun passes from Sagittarius (Dhanur) to Capricorn (Makar). The Sankranti is always thought to be a special time but the Makara Sankrati is very special indeed. Hindus believe that the **atman** or soul of anyone who dies on this day will go straight to be reunited with **Brahman** and escape **samsara** or the cycle of death and rebirth. Hindus celebrate this festival in different ways but they will always give alms (money) to charities or the poor and say sorry to anyone they have quarrelled with. They also give each other presents of sweets made with sesame seeds.

Kumbh Mela

Kumbh Mela takes place once every three years, with a special festival every twelve years. The time is fixed by the astrologers and depends on a certain line up of the planets. The festival lasts for several weeks and four Indian cities take turns to host it. These are the cities of Allahabad, Hardwar, Ujjain and Nasik. All these cities are next to **sacred** rivers and during the festival millions of worshippers bathe in the water. They believe that this washes away their sins and grants them **salvation**. This means they will no longer have to go through samsara but when they die they will be reunited with Brahman and achieve **moksha**.

A story about the festival of Kumbh Mela

The god Indra lost all his wealth and power when he was cursed by a holy man for being arrogant. The demon King Bali saw this as a chance to overcome the gods, but Vishnu told Indra that he needed to drink the nectar of the gods from the bottom of the ocean in order to regain his power and splendour.

After a great churning of the seas, the nectar was found, and the demons and gods fought a great battle over it. The gods finally won, and Vishnu gave the precious liquid to Garuda, the king of the birds, to carry back to a spiritual haven. The journey took Garuda twelve days, which was the equivalent of twelve human years. Along the way, he rested and put the container down. Some drops of the nectar were spilled at Allahabad, Ujjain and Nasik, which made them holy places forever.

Pilgrimage

In this section you will:
- learn about Hindu places of pilgrimage
- think about the reasons why people go on pilgrimages.

What is a pilgrimage?

A **pilgrimage** is a special religious journey and a form of worship. People who go on pilgrimages are called **pilgrims**. Pilgrims visit places they believe to be holy or **sacred**. They may travel on their own or with lots of other pilgrims.

Why do Hindus go on pilgrimages?

Most Hindus believe that making a pilgrimage is part of their **dharma**, or religious duty. They believe that visiting sacred places in this life will improve their **karma** and bring them rewards in the next life when they are reborn. Many Hindus believe that prayers said at sacred places they visit on a pilgrimage are more powerful than those said anywhere else.

Where do Hindus go on pilgrimage?

Pilgrimage sites are found all over India. Some of these places are important to all Hindus and others are important only to Hindus who worship a certain **deity**.

Pilgrimages can take weeks or months and the journey may cover hundreds or even thousands of miles. Many Hindus travel vast distances, for example Bombay to Varanasi is almost 1000 miles and Delhi to Tirupati, in the south east of the country, is much more than that. Some Hindus believe that suffering hardship on the journey is part of what it means to serve God and that they should walk all the way; others, however, travel by bus or train for much of the journey. Many Hindus join tours organized by travel agents to make their pilgrimage.

Varanasi

Varanasi, also known as Benares, is situated on the banks of the River **Ganges**. Hindus believe that Shiva, the god of destruction

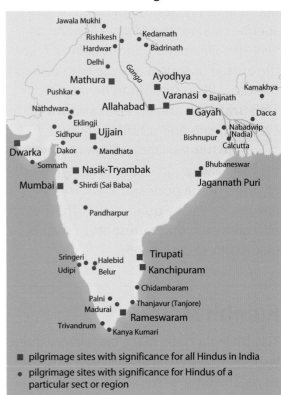

- ■ pilgrimage sites with significance for all Hindus in India
- • pilgrimage sites with significance for Hindus of a particular sect or region

A map of India showing some important pilgrimage sites

and re-creation, once lived there. Varanasi is also an important place for other religions and has been a centre for religious study and worship for thousands of years. Every year millions of Hindus visit this site to bathe in the sacred water to be made clean from all their sins. The banks of the river are lined with special platforms called ghats. These are used for **puja** and for **cremation**. Many Hindus hope to die at Varanasi and have their ashes scattered on the sacred river. They believe this will reunite them with Brahman and save them from **samsara**, the cycle of death and rebirth.

Vrindavan

Vrindavan is another sacred city. It is believed to be the birthplace of Krishna, the eighth **avatar** of Vishnu. There are more than 5000 **mandirs** dedicated to **Krishna** and pilgrims follow a special route around the city, chanting 'Hare Krishna' as they go.

Allahabad

Allahabad is where the sacred waters of the River Ganges and Jumna join together.

Every twelve years many millions of pilgrims make a pilgrimage to Allahabad to take part in ritual bathing as part of the festival of Kumbh Mela, believing that their sins will be washed away. In 1995, it was estimated that 17,000,000 Hindu pilgrims took part in this festival.

Rameswaram

Rameswaram, in southern India, is an important place of pilgrimage. It is one of the most sacred Hindu towns. According to Hindu legend, this is where Rama (an incarnation of Vishnu) and his wife Sita lived after she had been saved from the demon Ravana, who had kidnapped her. Legend says that Rama and Sita built a **shrine** here, dedicated to Shiva. They are said to have worshipped him in order to purify themselves from the sin of killing Ravana and to give thanks for their safe return.

Jagannath Puri

Puri, on the east coast of India, is an ancient pilgrimage site. Pilgrims come here to worship Lord Jagannath, also known as Vishnu, the Lord of the Universe. In the temple is a sacred wooden **murti** of Krishna, which is pulled through the streets on an chariot during some Hindu festivals.

A cremation by the banks of the River Ganges

Rites of passage 1

What are the Hindu rites of passage?

Rites of passage are special ceremonies that mark important stages in a person's life.

The life of a Hindu is divided into four main stages called **ashramas**. Each ashrama has religious rituals called **samskars**, which means 'making perfect'. There are sixteen samskars and very few people go through all the ceremonies. What must be done at each samskar is written in Hindu scripture.

The first samskar takes place before a child is conceived and the last one after death. Not all Hindus practise every one of the samskars. For some Hindus the time when the samskars are carried out varies.

Ashramas and samskars	
First ashrama – samskars 1–9	Starts before birth and relates to childhood
Second ashrama – samskars 10–12	Relates to youth
Third ashrama – samskars 13–15	Relates to responsibility, marriage and middle age
Fourth ashrama – samskar 16	Relates to old age and is carried out after death

First Ashrama

Three samskars take place before birth. The parents pray for a healthy baby and read parts of Hindu scripture to the foetus.

Jatakarman is the fourth samskar and takes place straight after birth before the umbilical cord is cut. The exact time of birth is written down and used to draw up a horoscope or **Janmapatri**.

Twelve days after birth the naming ceremony, called **Namakarana** samskar takes place. The priest advises which letter the child's name should begin with based on the Janmapatri. The family perform **puja** and prayers are said.

The sixth samskar takes place when the baby has its first outing. Prayers are said to protect the child from any evil.

The seventh samskar is when the baby eats solid food for the first time and the eighth when the child has its first haircut. This is usually done by the father and symbolizes the removal of any bad **karma**, **samchita karma**, which has been brought forward from a previous life.

The ninth samskar is when the child has its ears pierced. Prayers are said to protect the child from sickness and disease.

The eighth samskar: a child's first haircut

Ashramas

In modern times, the four ashramas, or stages of life, usually mean a change of lifestyle rather than a complete way of life:

● Brahamachari – the stage of studentship and religious study with a **guru**.

● Grihastha – the householder stage, including marriage and raising a family.

● Vanaprashta – the forest dweller. In times past, this meant retirement from work and time spent away from family to concentrate on spiritual matters.

● Sannyasa – the final stage of renunciation, when a Hindu leaves home after giving away everything they own. Traditionally, the rest of his life was spent wandering and thinking about God.

Rites of passage 2

In this section you will:

● learn more about Hindu rites of passage, including marriage and death

● read about the 'second birth' for Hindu boys

● read and reflect upon some Hindu marriage vows.

The sacred thread ceremony

The tenth **samskar** is very important to boys aged between eight and twelve years old who belong to the three highest social groups or **varnas**. This samskar is called the **upanayan**, which means 'getting closer to God' or the **sacred** thread ceremony. During the ceremony a

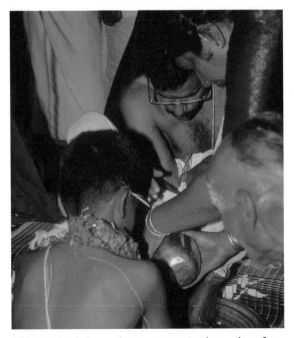

The sacred thread ceremony is thought of as a spiritual birth

sacred thread made of three strands is draped across the boy's left shoulder to hang down to his right hip. The three threads represent the three responsibilities or duties the boy now has. The first is to **Brahman**, the second is to his male ancestors, and the third is to his **guru** or spiritual teacher. The boy will wear the thread for the rest of his life, only changing it at festivals, to remind him of his **dharma** or religious duty as a Hindu. After the ceremony, boys are able to carry out religious ceremonies and they are expected to study the sacred writings with a guru.

Marriage

The thirteenth samskar takes place when Hindus get married. It is one of the oldest and most important rites of passage. At the beginning of the ceremony the bride and groom place garlands around each others necks as symbols of acceptance. They sit side by side under a canopy facing the priest. Prayers are said and **mantras** recited and the couple make symbolic offerings of wood, ghee (purified butter) and grains into a sacred fire. The bride and groom walk seven times around the fire while the priest, family and guests say prayers for their future happiness. For the first three rounds the bride leads the way and for the last four the groom leads the way. Then they take seven steps together facing north. At each step they pray for specific blessings such as happiness, strength, children and lifelong friendship. In Britain Hindus also take part in a civil ceremony to register the marriage as legal and binding.

A Hindu bride and groom sitting under a specially erected wedding canopy

Death

The sixteenth samskar takes place after death. Hindus believe that this rite of passage helps the **atman** to move to the next life or be reunited with God (**moksha**).

In India when someone dies the body is washed and wrapped in a large white piece of cloth called a shroud and placed on a stretcher to be carried to the **cremation** ground. The eldest son or male relative leads the procession, carrying a pot of water to use in the ceremony. The stretcher is placed on a funeral pyre. The eldest son or male relative walks around the pyre three times, sprinkling water, and then smashes the pot on the ground in front of where the head of the corpse lies. This symbolizes the release of the atman. Prayers are said and passages from sacred writings are read or recited. Sweet-smelling spices are thrown onto the funeral pyre, which is lit and left to burn.

Hindus like to be cremated near to one of India's sacred rivers or another source of running water so that when the mourners return they can gather up the ashes and scatter them onto the river. Nowadays many Hindus, especially those who live outside India, use modern crematoriums, but they want their ashes scattered in one of the sacred rivers such as the River **Ganges**. The family of the ex-Beatle George Harrison took his ashes to India to do this. After a Hindu funeral there is a period of mourning and families spend quiet time together. This usually lasts about ten days.

'Twice-born' Hindus

Between the ages of nine and twelve, Hindu boys take part in the sacred thread ceremony. Hindus believe that this is their second birth – a religious or spiritual birth, which signifies the start of their religious life and responsibilities. Boys are expected to respect their parents and their teachers, to study hard, and not to eat or drink anything which may harm them.

Vows at a wedding

These vows will be said during a Hindu wedding ceremony.

'Now with these seven steps, we are related as husband and wife and our bond is eternal. Let our love and friendship become eternal.
We have accepted each other in the presence of God, our ancestors, our parents, our relatives and friends; we will abide by our Vedic scriptures…'

Creation 1

In this section you will:

- learn what Hindus believe to be true about creation
- read some words from the Bhagavad Gita about creation.

Hindus believe that God, in the form of Brahma, is the creator of the universe and everything in it. However, they have different ideas about how creation actually happened. There are many ancient **myths** that describe unusual events and mysteries but nothing to say how everything began in the first place.

This passage from the **Vedas** helps many Hindus to accept that the creation is a mystery that no one knows the answer to:

Then even nothingness was not, nor existence.
There was no air then, nor the heavens beyond it.
Who covered it? Where was it? In whose keeping?
Was there then cosmic water, in depths unfathomed?
But, after all, who knows, and who can say,
Whence it all came, and how creation happened?
The gods themselves are later than creation,
So who knows when it truly has arisen?

Rig Veda, X, 129

One of the most well-known Hindu myths of creation is found in the Vedas. It says that everything in creation came about because of the sacrifice of the first man, **Purusha**.

All living creatures were made from the ghee (purified butter) that came from Purusha. The **deities** and the sun and the moon were also created. According to the myth, each part of Purusha created a different part of the universe. The atmosphere came from his navel, the heavens from his head, the earth from his feet, and the sky from his ear. Purusha is also responsible for the four **varnas** or social groups. The **Brahmins** (priests) came from his mouth, the **Kshatriyas** (rulers and soldiers) from his arms, the **Vaishyas** (shopkeepers, traders and farmers) from his thighs and the **Shudras** (servants) from his feet.

The Bhagavad Gita and creation

These words from the sacred **smirti** scripture – the **Bhagavad Gita** – explain Hindu beliefs about creation.

'I am the Father and the Mother of the world.'

Bhagavad Gita, 9, 17

'The Great Principle, the Divine, is in my womb;
I cast the seed into it:
There is the origin
of all creatures.
Whatever forms originate
In any wombs
The real womb is the Divine, the great Principle.'

Bhagavad Gita, 14, 4

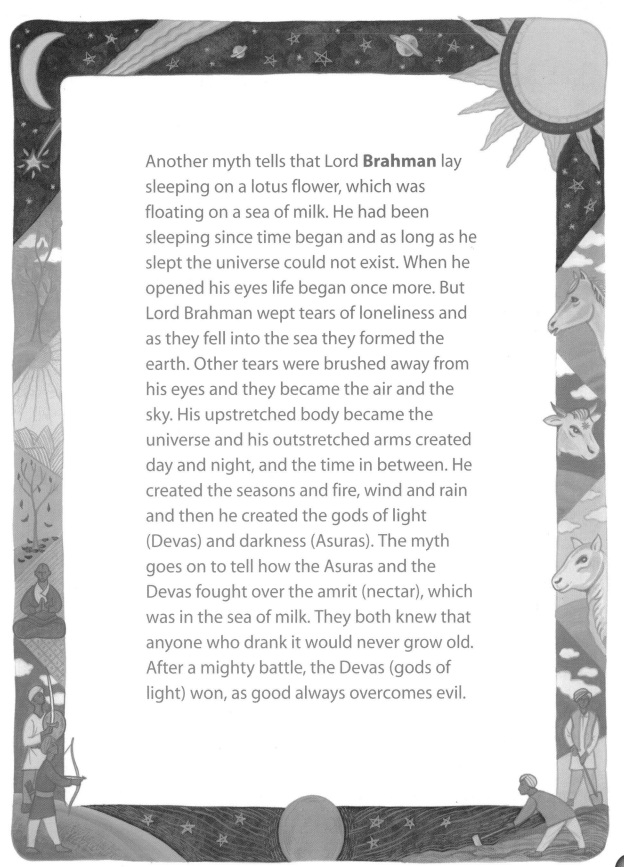

Another myth tells that Lord **Brahman** lay sleeping on a lotus flower, which was floating on a sea of milk. He had been sleeping since time began and as long as he slept the universe could not exist. When he opened his eyes life began once more. But Lord Brahman wept tears of loneliness and as they fell into the sea they formed the earth. Other tears were brushed away from his eyes and they became the air and the sky. His upstretched body became the universe and his outstretched arms created day and night, and the time in between. He created the seasons and fire, wind and rain and then he created the gods of light (Devas) and darkness (Asuras). The myth goes on to tell how the Asuras and the Devas fought over the amrit (nectar), which was in the sea of milk. They both knew that anyone who drank it would never grow old. After a mighty battle, the Devas (gods of light) won, as good always overcomes evil.

Creation 2

In this section you will:

- learn more about Hindu beliefs about creation
- find out about the attitude of Hindus towards the environment
- read about the work of the Chipko movement in protecting India's forests.

The avatars of Vishnu

Hindus believe that the god Vishnu, the preserver of the universe, has visited earth in nine different forms (**avatars**). Some Hindus believe that these avatars can help to explain creation and **evolution**.

What is the Hindu attitude towards the environment?

The earth provides enough to satisfy everyone's needs, but not everyone's greed.

Mahatma Gandhi

Hindus believe that everything on earth is a gift from God and all human beings should show respect and live in harmony with nature. Many natural places, such as mountains and rivers, are thought to be holy and trees are also **sacred**. Many religious rituals surround cutting and planting trees. When a tree has to be cut down, it is asked to forgive the woodcutter before this is done. Some Hindus believe that **deities** live in trees during the rainy season. Many Hindus are environmentalists. They work hard to care for the world and its resources and believe that a balance should be kept between what is taken from the earth and what is put back into it.

The Chipko movement

'What do the forest's bear? Soil, water and pure air.'

Chipko movement motto

Hindu scriptures emphasize that we must look after nature. The forests in India are also important for people who live in rural areas, because they provide fuel, food and animal fodder. However, in modern times, forests have been cut down to make way for industry. Many Hindus have protested against this deforestation.

A group called the Chipko movement has been very successful. In 1980, they succeeded in obtaining a fifteen-year ban on cutting down living trees in the Himalayas. They have also strongly influenced the Indian government's policy on using natural resources, and have made politicians more aware of the needs of rural people.

The supporters of the Chipko movement are mainly village women, although some men have been involved, too. They have used a passive form of resistance to save the forests – they hugged the trees so that they could not be cut down.

1 Hindu scripture says the first avatar of Vishnu was as a giant fish called Matysa. He came after a previous creation of human beings had all been drowned in a flood because of their wicked ways. The only survivors were the king and seven sages or wise men and their families. They had taken refuge in an ark along with males and females of many different animals. Matysa towed the ark across the sea to a place of safety and a new creation began.

10 Hindus believe that there is a tenth avatar of Vishnu yet to come – Kalki. They think he will recreate the world.

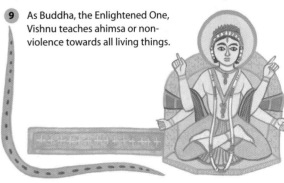

2 As Kurma, a giant tortoise, Vishnu carried a giant mountain on his back. This was used to help the deities to churn the seas to search for ambrosia, the divine nectar, which was needed to restore the power to the gods. The festival of Kumbh Mela celebrates this event.

9 As Buddha, the Enlightened One, Vishnu teaches ahimsa or non-violence towards all living things.

3 As Varaha, a giant boar, Vishnu saved the earth from a second flood. He lifted the earth up out of the water on his giant tusks.

8 As Krishna, Vishnu had many wonderful adventures which encourages his followers to carry out their dharma or religious duties.

4 As Narasimha, half man and half lion, Vishnu kills Hiranyaksipu, who was torturing his son, Prahlad. Vishnu became half man and half lion and killed him with his nails, because he could not be killed by any animal, human or weapon.

7 As Rama, Vishnu defeated a ten-headed demon called Ravana. This is celebrated at the festivals of Divali and Dassehra.

5 As Vamana, a dwarf, Vishnu saved the gods from a demon king called Bali. He tricked Bali into agreeing to give him three steps of land but then he expanded his size so that the steps took in the whole universe.

6 As Parasurama, Vishnu saved the earth from wicked kings who were abusing their power and not following religious teachings.

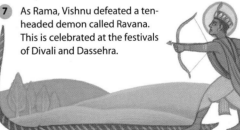

The avatars of Vishnu

In this section you will:

● learn how Hindus decide what is right and what is wrong

● find out about Hindu attitudes to animal rights, including vivisection.

A Hindu will often talk to their priest or guru before making an important decision

What is a moral issue?

Communities have laws, religious beliefs and teachings, and shared values, which guide the decisions made by the people and the actions they take. Morality is about right and wrong actions and behaviours based on these ideas. The word 'immoral' means 'wrong'. If someone does something that is immoral this means that they have chosen to act in a way that is seen by the community to be wrong. Someone who is amoral shows no understanding about what is right and what is wrong.

How do Hindus decide what is right wrong?

Hindus try to live their lives the way **Brahman** wants them to. They believe that the experiences of **deities** and holy men can show them the right way to live.

Just try to learn the truth by approaching a spiritual master. Inquire from him submissively and render service unto him. The self-realized souls can impart knowledge to you, because they have seen the truth.

Bhagavad Gita, 4, 34

Sacred writings are a source of moral authority for Hindus. This means they tell them what is the morally right thing to do. This advice is given through stories about what deities have done when faced with problems and they also contain important teaching about the right way to behave. When making a difficult decision, many Hindus think about what their special deity would do and they pray to them for help and advice. They may also talk to their guru or priest or discuss the problem with other Hindus.

Hindus also think about the effect of their actions and whether this will bring good or bad **karma**. Hindus believe that all thoughts and actions have consequences. This means that their behaviour in one lifetime is rewarded or punished in the next. If they have lived a good life in this lifetime, in the next lifetime they will be one stage nearer to **moksha**, when they will be reunited with Brahman. If they have not lived a good life, they will be one stage further away from moksha and the next life will not be as good as this one.

Because of their beliefs Hindus face moral dilemmas such as, is abortion acceptable and should we care for the poor and needy or do they deserve to be as they are?

Hindus must accept the consequences of their action to their karma and in reality many Hindus work tirelessly to help others whatever their need. The abortion rate in India has increased considerably in modern times.

Brahman, God, gives life to all living creatures and only God has the right to end that life. For Hindus this means having respect for all living things. A lot of Hindus are vegetarians because of this belief.

Hindus also treat animals with respect because they believe there is part of Brahman in every living thing. In human beings and animals this is the **atman** or soul.

What do Hindus think about animal rights?

Hinduism teaches that the greatest **dharma** or religious duty is to practise **ahimsa**. Ahimsa means 'not killing' or 'non-violence'. Hindus believe that

*Hindus believe that the cow is a sacred animal. The **Vedas** state that it is forbidden to kill cows*

Vivisection

Hindus believe that God is present in all living creatures, and this influences how they feel about medical research. Mahatma Gandhi (1869–1948) expressed very strong opinions about vivisection, which involves hurting living animals during scientific research. These views are shared by many Hindus today.

'Vivisection is the blackest of all the black crimes that a man is at present committing against God and his fair creation. It ill becomes us to invoke in our daily prayers the blessings of God, the Compassionate, if we in turn will not practise elementary compassion towards our fellow creatures. I abhor vivisection with my whole soul. All the scientific discoveries stained with innocent blood I count as of no consequence.'

Mahatma Gandhi

In this section you will:

- ● learn how Hindus believe people should treat each other
- ● find out about Hindu attitudes towards prejudice and discrimination.

Prejudice and discrimination

Prejudice means you make a judgement or form an opinion about someone without any real evidence. Discrimination is when, because of your prejudice, you treat some people better or worse than others. There are many different kinds of prejudice and people are discriminated against for many different reasons such as colour, race, religion, size, gender, accent, and so on. Discrimination on the grounds of race or colour is called racism. Treating everyone the same is called equality.

Prejudice can lead to stereotyping. This means that you have a fixed idea about what a particular group of people are like or how they will all behave.

How do Hindus believe people should treat each other?

Hindus may greet each other with their palms and fingers pressed together whilst making a small bow from the waist as a sign of respect. This traditional greeting is called 'namaste', which means

'I honour that place within you where **Brahman** resides'. This symbolizes the Hindu belief that all human beings should be treated with respect because their **atman** that is within them is part of Brahman.

Hinduism is very tolerant of other religions and races. However, because of the way in which the **varnas** or social groups are organized, and the **caste system**, they have not always treated each other with respect and this has sometimes led to inequality, prejudice and discrimination within the religion.

Prejudice and discrimination has been one of the most difficult issues for Hindus in India to deal with. Centuries of tradition which did not give equality to women and valued boy babies more than girls has been hard to change. Parents wanted a boy baby because traditionally boys stay with their families and support their parents in their old age whereas girls leave to go and live with their husband's family.

Mahatma Gandhi

Mahatma Gandhi was a very important Hindu leader who believed that people should not be discriminated against because of their religion. He campaigned to change the attitude of people towards the caste system and improve the lives of millions of Indian Hindus called the **untouchables**. These were the least important group of people, who had to do all the dirty jobs that no one else would do. He renamed them **harijans**, which means 'children of God'. Gandhi set up an **ashram**, a community for spiritual families had always done. This still happens to some extent in modern India but Hindus who live in other countries do many different jobs and marry outside of their own caste. In India the untouchables now call themselves **dalits**, which means 'the oppressed'. They have formed a political party and campaign for greater equality.

Mahatma Gandhi outside the Sabarmati Ashram, Ahmedabad, India

development, where Hindus of all castes and harijans lived and worked together.

Mine is not a religion of the prison house. It has room for the least among God's creations. But it has proof against insolence, pride of race, religion and colour.

Mahatma Gandhi

In 1948, because of Gandhi's long campaign, a law was finally passed by the Indian government, to ban 'untouchability' and this was followed by other laws on equality.

In the past, Hindus could only mix with members of their own **jati** or caste. They could not marry anyone from a different caste, and could only do jobs which their

Dr B. R. Ambedkar (1891–1956)

Bhimji Ramji Ambedkar was born into the lowest varna, or caste (previously known as the 'untouchables', but now called 'dalits'). He suffered discrimination throughout his life because of his varna. At school, he was separated from higher caste students, but he was determined to succeed. As a successful lawyer, upper caste employees would not give him access to information or allow him to drink from the same source as them.

He started an organization to fight for equality, so that untouchables had proper education and better jobs. The organization campaigned to remove the discrimination which prevented untouchables going into a temple or drawing water from public wells and tanks.

Ambedkar started the dalit political party in 1947. He was responsible for chairing the committee which drafted the constitution of India. The constitution proclaims equality for all citizens. Dalits consider Dr Ambedkar to be their liberator and champion.

Ultimate questions 1

In this section you will:

● find out what Hindus think about some of life's mysteries, including the existence of God

● gain an understanding of how Hindus view abortion.

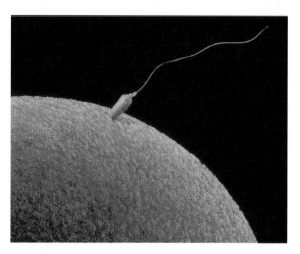

A new life begins – an egg and sperm at the point of fertilization

What is an ultimate question?

Ultimate questions are usually about something that is difficult to explain or prove such as, 'How did everything begin?' or 'Does God exist?' People often ask ultimate questions to try to make sense of the world in which they live or to help find meaning and purpose to their lives. There are no definite answers to ultimate questions. The way people respond will depend on their view of the world and their religious beliefs. Many people believe that the existence of God can explain many of the things that puzzle them.

Hinduism teaches that asking questions is an important part of a person's spiritual development. Many Hindus believe that asking questions and seeking the truth about God and their place in the world is a very important part of their religious life.

Why do we exist?

Hindus believe that all life is **sacred** because it comes as a precious gift from God. They say we exist because God has chosen to give us life. The Hindu belief in the sanctity of life is shown as **ahimsa**, which means not harming any living creature by thought, word or deed. This belief affects what Hindus think about a lot of issues such as genetic engineering, embryo technology, abortion and euthanasia.

What are we here for?

Hindus believe that **gurus**, or spiritual teachers, 'awaken' them so that they understand their true purpose on earth, which is to develop and show their love for God. To do this they must carry out their religious duty or **dharma** and this includes helping and caring for other people. Giving loving service to God and humans is called **seva** and is the highest form of dharma. Seva also includes worshipping regularly and supporting charities and good causes. Hindus believe it can produce good **karma**, which will help them to achieve **moksha** and be reunited with God.

Hindus helping each other at a community health programme in Rajasthan, India

What happens when we die?

For to one that is born death is certain
And birth is certain for one that has died;
Therefore, the thing being unavoidable,
Thou shouldst not mourn.

Bhagavad Gita 2, 27

Hindus believe that the **atman** is eternal, which means it lives forever. When a Hindu dies the atman will be reborn in another form, which depends on the karma they have 'earned' during previous lifetimes on earth. Hinduism teaches that every living being has a relationship with God. They call this **svarupa**. It may take

many lifetimes before the atman is pure enough to be reunited with God and not reborn. Hindus see this as a welcome release from the suffering they may experience during life on earth.

Abortion

Hinduism teaches that abortion is one of the greatest sins (maha-papa). It goes completely against the Hindu belief in ahimsa, or non-violence. Hindus believe that, unless the mothers' health is seriously at risk, abortion cannot be justified.

Hindu scripture says that life begins at conception. This is when the atman (soul) enters the developing foetus – although some Hindus do not believe that the atman 'wakes up' until about the 28th week of pregnancy. The unborn baby is regarded as a living being, separate from its mother, and that it must be protected and respected.

Hindus accept that life on earth can be difficult, but they believe that life is still very valuable. Hinduism teaches that the atman must have the chance to experience this life. It should have the opportunity to escape **samsara**, the cycle of life and death, and become united with God. However, nowadays, abortion is becoming more common for Hindus in India and elsewhere.

Ultimate questions 2

In this section you will:

● find out about how Hindus respond to evil and suffering in the world

● read about the work of the Swaminarayan movement.

Where does suffering come from?

There are many different causes of suffering. Sometimes suffering is the result of a natural disaster, such as an earthquake or flooding. Natural disasters are not human made.

Suffering is also caused through deliberate acts of violence, such as murder, terrorism and war. These are acts of moral evil because they are wrong or wicked.

Sometimes suffering is caused accidentally by thoughtlessness or by abusing natural resources.

What is the Hindu response to suffering?

Hindus believe that pain and suffering are as a result of bad **karma** in a previous lifetime. Karma is the concept that all thoughts and actions have consequences, which are carried forward to the next life.

Refugees receiving hospitality in a Hindu community in Charlestown, South Africa

It is seen as the ultimate justice for good or bad behaviour. Nevertheless, Hindus find pain and suffering difficult to deal with. Every Hindu wants to achieve **moksha** so they no longer have to be reborn and accept the consequences of their previous life.

The Ramakrishna Vedanta Mission

Hindus see trying to help those who are suffering or in pain as part of their **dharma** or religious duty. In India, the Ramakrishna Vedanta Mission was founded to provide social services and spiritual development for the poor. The motto of the organization is 'Liberation for oneself and service to mankind'.

The Ramakrishna Vedanta Mission has its own hospitals, clinics and mobile dispensaries taking medicine to rural areas. It runs homes for the elderly and orphanages, as well as having its own schools for all ages of pupils and those with physical disabilities. The Mission runs adult training centres and teacher training institutes and also provides relief for people when natural disasters such as famine or earthquakes occur.

The Swaminarayan movement

The Swaminarayan movement is a Hindu group, or **denomination**, which is committed to the worship of Vishnu. Under the leadership of Pujya Pramukh Swami Maharaja, the movement has grown into an international welfare organization. It is linked to the United Nations, and it runs hospitals, schools, youth hospitals and medical camps.

Pramukh Swami is also committed to building temples, in order to bring people closer to God so that they will want to help others. He says:

'Temples are also hospitals and universities for the treatment and education of one's soul. Millions of people find peace in temples, which they do not find in cinemas, restaurants and discos – or even in their own homes.'

The Ramakrishna Vedanta Mission logo

Glossary

Ahimsa 'not killing', 'non-violence'; a reverence and respect for all life

Arti a religious ceremony during which love and devotion is offered to the deity and the worshippers believe they receive blessings in return

Asceticism choosing to live a simple and harsh life for religious reasons

Ashram a community set up for spiritual development

Ashrama a stage of life, of which there are four

Atman the soul or 'real self', a part of God which is in all living beings

Aum/Om a sacred sound and symbol which represents God

Avatar 'one who descends'; refers to the appearance or incarnation of a deity on earth, usually Vishnu

Bhagavad Gita 'The Song of the Lord'; part of the Mahabharata, believed to have been spoken by Krishna, and one of the most popular Hindu sacred texts

Bhagavad Purana a collection of twelve books containing information about the avatars of Vishnu and famous stories about Krishna

Bhajans devotional hymns or songs

Brahmin the first of the four varnas. Priests come from this varna

Camphor an aromatic substance believed to have antiseptic properties. It is burnt and used as a disinfectant in order to cleanse and purify the air around a place of prayer such as a shrine

Caste a sub-group within a varna made up of numerous families who follow the same occupation. Also known as a jati

Caste system the organization of Indian society into occupational kinship groups

Cremation the burning of a dead body

Dalit 'the oppressed'; a name adopted by Hindus who are outside the caste system. They are also known as 'untouchables' or harijans ('children of God')

Deity a god or goddess

Denomination a group within Hinduism

Dharma religious duty – right conduct

Diva a small clay oil-filled lamp with a floating wick, used at the festival of Divali

Divali the festival of lights which commemorates the Hindu New Year

Divine godlike

Evolution the gradual and natural development of the universe over a long period of time

Fast to stop eating all or certain foods, especially for religious reasons

Finite limited, not lasting forever

Ganges also known as 'Ganga', the most famous of all the sacred rivers in India

Guru a spiritual teacher, also known as a sadhu, swami or holy man

Hare Krishna Movement the International Society of Krishna Consciousness (ISKCON)

Harijans 'children of God'; a name given by Gandhi for the 'untouchables'

Havan the ceremony at which ghee and grains are made into fire

Hermit a person who lives in solitude

Hinduism a major world religion, also known as Sanatan Dharma, the eternal or imperishable religion

Janmapatri a horoscope chart drawn up by an astrologer, usually for a newborn baby

Jati a sub-group within a varna made up of numerous families who follow the same occupation. Also known as a caste

Karma 'action'; the law of cause and effect. The belief that all thoughts and actions have results that correspond to them

Kshatriyas the second of the four varnas, made up of rulers and soldiers

Laws of Manu a collection of sacred books which contain rules about how Hindus should live their lives

Lotus flower a flower used as a symbol to represent purity and goodness

Mahabharata the world's longest poem; a sacred text also known as the Great Indian Epic, which includes the Bhagavad Gita

Mala a string of wooden prayer beads used in meditation, also known as a rosary

Mandir a Hindu place of worship, also known as a temple

Mantra a short religious saying or prayer which Hindus chant regularly as part of their worship

Meditation a form of quiet prayer which involves clearing the mind of all distractions and concentrating on God

Moksha liberation or freedom from samsara

Murti an image or representation of a deity

Myths ancient stories about mysterious events, unusual traditions or extraordinary sights in nature

Namakarana the Hindu naming ceremony

Omnipotent all-powerful

Omnipresent always present, everywhere

Omniscient all-knowing

Pilgrim a person who goes on a religious journey or pilgrimage

Pilgrimage a religious journey

Prashad sacred or sanctified food

Puja worship carried out by Hindus at home or in the mandir

Puranas a collection of Hindu sacred texts which contain stories about Brahma, Vishnu and Shiva, and teachings about morality. The most important Purana is the Bhagavad Purana

Rakhi a bracelet made out of coloured cotton or silk, given as a symbol of gratitude and protection

Ramayana a sacred text in the form of a poem, which tells the story of Rama and Sita

Rangoli repetitive, geometrical patterns which are painted in coloured powder, a traditional art of India

Rashi a sign of the Hindu zodiac

Reincarnation samsara; the cycle of birth, death and rebirth

Sacred holy, associated with God

Salvation moksha; liberation from samsara

Samchita karma the combined consequences of a person's thoughts and actions which are carried over from one lifetime to another

Samsara reincarnation; the cycle of birth, death and rebirth

Samskars sixteen religious ceremonies which mark important stages in a Hindu's life

Sanatan Dharma the eternal or imperishable religion, also known as Hinduism

Sanskrit one of the world's oldest languages

Seva service, either to God or to mankind

Shaivas people who worship Shiva as the Supreme God

Shaktas people who worship Shakta, the wife of Shiva, in one of her various forms, such as Durga or Kali, as the Supreme God

Shakti the destructive and reproductive energy associated with Shiva, which usually takes the form of a female deity

Shrine a special place set aside for worship

Shruti 'that which is heard'; a category of sacred writing which is believed to have been composed by God

Shudras the lowest of the four varnas, made up of unskilled workers

Smriti 'that which has been remembered'; a category of sacred writing which is believed to have been composed by human beings

Svarupa a term used to describe the eternal relationship between living beings and God

Swami a spiritual teacher, also known as a guru, sadhu or holy man

Swastika 'well-being'; a favourable Hindu symbol which represents good fortune and happiness

Transmigration the belief that the atman, or soul, survives after death and enters a new body

Trimurti the three main forms of God: Brahma (the creator), Vishnu (the preserver) and Shiva (the destroyer)

Upanayan 'sacred thread ceremony'; the tenth samskar. A very important religious ceremony for boys who belong to the three highest varnas

Upanishads sacred text that explains the teachings of the Vedas

Vaishnavas people who worship Vishnu and his avatars as the Supreme God

Vaishyas the third of the four varnas, made up of merchants (shopkeepers and traders) and farmers

Varnas four classes or groups which make up traditional Indian society

Vedas 'to know', 'knowledge'; a collection of shruti, 'divinely given writings'. The oldest and most important Hindu sacred writings

Index

Abortion 57
Ahimsa 25, 53, 56
Ambedkar, Dr B. R. 55
Animal rights 53
Arti 34–5
Ash 30
Ashramas 45
Atman 10, 24, 47, 57
Aum 28, 31

Bhagavad Gita 12–13
Bhajans 34, 35
Bindi 30
Brahma 12, 14, 15, 48
Brahman 4, 14
Brahmins 26, 27, 48, 49

Caste 26, 27, 55
Chaturthi 39
Chipko movement 50
Coconut 29
Creation 48–9

Dassehra 39
Death 47, 57
Denominations 4, 8
Dharma 13, 22, 24, 30, 32, 42, 56
Discrimination 54
Divali 13, 38
Durga 5, 17, 20, 39

Environment 50

Gandhi, Mahatma 50, 53, 54–5
Ganesha 19, 21, 32
Ganges 31, 41, 43
Guru 4, 22–3, 25

Havan 35
Holi 39
Horoscope chart see Janmapatri

ISKCON 6–7, 8

Jagannath Puri 43
Janmapatri 37, 44

Janmashtami 40
Jati 26, 27, 55

Kali 5, 17, 20
Karma 24, 27, 42, 45, 53, 57
    samchita karma 27
Kathakali 33
Krishna 4, 6, 8, 12, 16, 18, 19, 40, 43, 51
Kshatriyas 26, 27, 48, 49
Kumbh Mela 41

Lakshmi 5, 21, 38
Laws of Manu 12
Lotus flower 29

Mahabharata 12–13
Makara Sankranti 41
Mandir 22, 34
Mantras 7, 32
Marriage 46–7
Meditation 25, 32
Moksha 23, 24, 25, 27, 41, 57
Mother Goddess 19, 39
Murti 15, 32

Navaratri 38–9

Om see Aum

Parvati 5, 17, 19, 20, 21
Prashad 35
Prayer 32
Prejudice 54
Priests 22
Puja 32–3, 34
Puja tray 33
Puranas 12
Purusha 27, 28, 29

Rakhi 40
Raksha Bandhan 40–1
Rama 8, 16, 18, 39, 51
Ramayana 13, 18, 39
Rameswaram 43
Reincarnation 24

Sacred thread ceremony
    see Upanayana

Samchita karma 27, 45, 57, 58
Samsara 24, 41, 43, 57
Samskar 44–7
Sanatan Dharma 2, 11, 22, 24, 32
Sanskrit 9
Saraswati 5, 20
Sathya Sai Baba 23
Seva 56–7
Shaivism 5
Shaktas 5
Shakti 17, 19, 20
Shiva 5, 8, 12, 14, 16–17, 19
Shiva linga 17
Shruti 8, 10–11
Shudras 26, 27, 48, 49
Sindoora 30
Sita 39
Smriti 8, 9, 12–13
Soul see Atman
Storytelling 22
Suffering 58
Swaminarayan movement 59
Swastika 28–9

Tilaka 31
Trimurti 14–17, 29

Untouchables 27, 55
Upanayana 46

Vaishnavism 4, 8
Vaishyas 26, 27, 48, 49
Varanasi 43
Varnas 12, 26
Vedas 10–11, 15, 32, 48, 53
Vishnu 4, 8, 12, 14, 16, 18, 21, 51
    avatars of 18, 50, 51
Vrindavan 43

Worship
    at home 32–3
    in the mandir 34–5

Yoga 22, 25